Wild Life

Also by Pat Neal

WildLife Volume 1
The Fisherman's Prayer

Wild Life

Volume 2

The Mountain Pond

Pat Neal

iUniverse, Inc.
New York   Bloomington

WildLife, Volume 2
The Mountain Pond

Copyright © 2009 Pat Neal

iUniverse books may be ordered through booksellers or by contacting:

iUniverse
1663 Liberty Drive
Bloomington, IN 47403
www.iuniverse.com
1-800-Authors (1-800-288-4677)

ISBN: 978-1-4401-4552-0 (pbk)
ISBN: 978-1-4401-4550-6 (cloth)
ISBN: 978-1-4401-4551-3 (ebook)

Printed in the United States of America

iUniverse rev. date: 6/19/09

Dedication

For my Father, Duane W. Neal
who showed me the Olympic Mountains

Epigraph

"And Adam gave names to all cattle and to all the fowl of the air and to every beast of the field."

Genesis 2:20

Contents

List of Illustrations

Author's Note

These stories may have appeared as newspaper columns in various newspapers in Washington State.

Introduction

It is daylight in the northern foothills of the Olympic Mountains. On a narrow bench above a wild river a mountain pond sits by the edge of a meadow. In the gray mist of morning, there is the outline of a shack on the edge of the timber. The windows are dark. There is no smoke coming from the chimney. The place appears as empty as the day I found it while wandering in the woods.

The mountain pond was formed at the end of the last ice age. The ice sheet blocked the river and flooded the land. The ice melted. The waters receded. The pond remained. The first people came to the pond about 14,000 years ago. They came to ambush animals by the pond—mastodon, caribou and bison. They left stone tools and cracked bones as a sign that they lived here.

The Salish people ventured upriver following deer and elk up into the mountains. They gathered bulbs, picked berries and medicinal plants. They stripped cedar bark for fabric. They left charcoal and heat-fractured rocks as a sign they lived here.

Later the land was settled by homesteaders who came looking for the last frontier. They built cabins, planted orchards and left rusty iron implements as a sign they once lived here.

It seems as only yesterday I came into this land. There was a homestead overgrown and empty. I chopped back the brush, planted a garden and dug out the well. I found the signs and felt the presence of those who had passed before. It was lonely in the silence of the haunted valley. I made friends with the birds and animals the old-fashioned way. I stopped shooting them.

After a year or so, I gained the trust of a great blue heron. He was the watchdog of the swamp, making a big racket if anything was amiss. Once Old Bill trusted me, the rest of the birds and animals seemed to lose their fear. There were skunks in the woodpile, squirrels in the living room and a bear that made a horrendous mess on the lawn. Migrating waterfowl would be blown off course and drop into the mountain pond to find a welcome refuge among a corrupt pack of ravens and jays. Elk and deer came by to raise their young and pillage the garden. Predators killed and ate their meals right outside my window. It was good, too good to last. The land was being settled. The wildlife had to go and so did I.

As I stood in the doorway on that final morning, the voices of the forest awoke. There was the cooing of the band-tailed pigeons, the hooting of the blue grouse and a guttural squawk from Old Bill, a sign of danger coming. I said goodbye to my friends. These stories are a sign that I lived here.

Spring Chores

Springtime was my favorite time of year in the hills. On a clear blue morning, the snow-capped Olympic Mountains seemed to stand so tall they could have fallen over, but they didn't. Although I was never one to stand around and enjoy the view when there were chores to do.

Springtime on the homestead meant that even though the days were getting longer, there still were not enough hours in the day to get all the chores done. I had to prioritize, delegate, and move on. I didn't set myself up for a lot of unrealistic expectations. When it came to chores on the homestead, the sooner you realized your expectations were unrealistic the better.

It is an eternal truth that you need the right tools for the job. Archaeologists tell us that man has been a tool user for over a million years. Recent advances in radiocarbon dating have determined that many of those tools were borrowed. In the course of human evolution, whoever borrowed the most tools ruled. Inevitably, early man gathered into walled cities to make beer and over the centuries, tools became more advanced. This may or may not be related. Anthropologists have theorized that the more advanced the tool, the greater the likelihood it was borrowed.

Take my shovel, please. It was one of the most highly evolved tools

I owned. I needed one to spade the garden. Too bad some worthless clam digger borrowed my shovel and never brought it back. That was OK. I've never been able to find a shovel that fit my hand anyway.

I had to prioritize, delegate, and move on to the next chore.

Springtime was way past time to split and stack the firewood rounds I had cut the winter before. I wanted to split the wood and get it properly seasoned so that it would burn without causing a chimney fire. Unless my axe handle was loose. Go splitting wood with a loose axe handle and you are asking for trouble. The axe head could fly off at any time, endangering myself and others.

It was safety first at all times on the homestead. I had to soak that axe handle so that it would swell up and fit tight in the axe head, and that was not a job you could rush.

Prioritize, delegate, and move on.

By then, it was way past time to mow the lawn, except for one thing. The dandelions were in bloom. That meant the honeybees were working the blossoms. Honeybees were nearly extirpated from their range by parasites and disease. It was a lucky miracle when a swarm of honeybees moved into a hole in the wall under the eaves of the house. I could listen to them buzz at all hours, making money while I slept.

I wasn't one to jerk the welcome mat out from under the bees by mowing the dandelions before they went to seed.

There was no way I was going to mow the dandelions after they went to seed, if I wanted to call myself a bird watcher. Our Washington State Bird, the goldfinch, gathers the dandelions' downy seeds to line their nests. I wasn't about to sacrifice unborn generations of state birds on the altar of bourgeois sensibilities just to mow the lawn.

That's life on the homestead. We work with the rhythm of the seasons to sit back on the porch at the end of the day and watch the axe handle soak.

The Blue Grouse

It was daylight in the swamp on a cool spring morning. I was listening to the silence.

Silence is said to be the rarest thing on earth. Nowhere is that more true than in the foothills of the Olympic Mountains in the spring. At first, the silence is broken only by the persistent whine of the great northern mosquito. These monstrous pests suck up great gushers of blood from any bare hide brave enough to show itself in the woods. Once the bugs show up, it's only a matter of time before the other plague appears—the frogs.

I heard there was a worldwide shortage of frogs. I thought it was because most every frog in the world was at my swamp. That's what it sounded like. The frogs croaked so loud it was almost like a roar, and then they would be silent all at once. That usually meant Old Bill was around. He was a great blue heron. It took me years to be his friend, although we were never very close.

At first, Bill would spook out of the pond, squawking like a terrorized dinosaur every time he saw me. I tried to talk to Bill and calm him down, repeating the words, "Land, land, land," three times in a lowering voice. Eventually, Bill—one of the wariest birds you ever saw—wouldn't fly off his perch when he saw me. If he was in flight, Bill would come in for a landing if I told him too.

Meanwhile, other creatures were listening and watching me and Old Bill. Once I gained Bill's trust, other herons would fly in for a landing. Bill found a mate shortly after the frogs woke up. They spent their days stalking the swamp in their breeding plumage, spearing frogs with their scimitar beaks, then cutting them up and choking them down. Or they would sit in the trees and croak at each other.

Toward evening, the herons would fly up to a timbered ridge top where they had a nest the size of a truck bed atop a spindly little hemlock.

To the wild creatures, the presence of a great blue heron meant safety. Two herons meant a party. Other birds flew in to investigate.

The belted kingfisher is a ridiculous looking bird with a head too big for its body and a beak too big for its head. It has an annoying habit of hovering in midair in a manner totally against the laws of physics, while making a racket of a call that sounds like a can full of rocks being shaken by an idiot.

People told me to shoot the kingfishers because they ate fish; but mine ate frogs, which made them okay in my book.

At least the kingfishers provided some amusement. Other species had no redeeming social value. Watching the yellow-bellied sapsucker, with its garish red and yellow feathers, its drunken attempts at flight, and a pathetic call that sounded like a rusty hinge, it's easy to see how they may have reached an evolutionary dead end.

Sapsuckers normally drill holes in trees to suck sap, of course. In the spring, they pound their heads against any and all available sheet metal to produce a rapping sound that can be heard a mile. The brain damage caused by the constant impact of the birds' skulls against metal could be a significant factor in their decline.

Until the unfortunate creatures went extinct, I was forced to listen to them beating on the roof for months on end. This was often accompanied by the drumming of the ruffed grouse, who has an odd habit of standing on a log and flapping its wings. This produces a call that sounds like someone trying to jump-start a helicopter. Just when you think you can't take it any more the blue grouse start hooting.

The call of the blue grouse sounds like the bass line on a boom box stuck on the same track from March through July. The male blue grouse produces this low hooting call with a pair of yellow inflatable air sacs on either side of its neck.

This droning mating call is accompanied by a nervous form of dance where the posturing males fan out their tail feathers, arch out their wings, and strut around in drunken half-circles like they are having a seizure.

It is at this stage of the mating behavior that the male blue grouse can become belligerent. There's a story about a blue grouse that attacked a log truck parked too long in the wrong place. A flurry of vicious wing-slaps against the truck tires left the driver uninjured, except for the emotional scars, which might never heal.

It's just this sort of thing that got people calling male blue grouse "hooters."

The only thing more pathetic than the mating ritual of the hooters is the sad fact it actually works. Even worse, I am watching them.

After weeks of interminable hooting, the female blue grouse inevitably appears. In contrast to the hooter's colorful plumage, the female's drab camouflage of brown feathers looks like something the cat dragged in.

The female grouse has been called a "fool hen" by people that don't know any better. They have never been attacked, as I have, by a nesting mother grouse. Few have and survived to tell about it.

This is my story:

One day I was out in the forest cutting wood when I heard a menacing clucking sound. There she was, big mother grouse with blood in her eye. Her feathers were all puffed up and turned the wrong way.

She struck without warning. She flew at my head—just missing by inches—and then landed in a heap a few feet away. It looked as if her wing was broken. I walked over to see if she needed help, and she jumped up, fluttered a few more feet, and crashed again.

I was too smart to fall for the old broken wing trick, where she decoys the vermin away from her chicks by pretending to be injured.

And yet, I couldn't help wondering if she didn't really get hurt trying to take me out. The woods are a dangerous place. Maybe it was her cry for help. I followed a long way into the brush, and her wing didn't seem to be getting any better.

The shadows lengthened. It was getting dark. I sat and listened to the silence of the forest.

The Swamp Kitty

It was daylight in the swamp. Something had gone terribly wrong. My head was pounding. My eyes were burning. My nose felt like it was on fire. Once again, I questioned the sanity of having a pet skunk. My life had been going a whole lot better without one.

We met on the day I rescued her, trapped in the bottom of a garbage can. She was snacking on an ice cream container. I called her "Kitty." She seemed to calm down when I got her more ice cream. The plan was to stuff Kitty so full of ice cream she could barely wiggle, and release her back into the swamp.

It turned out all the ice cream in the world would not have calmed Kitty down enough to stuff a cork in it long enough to make it out to the swamp. Kitty let loose with a corrosive fog. I dropped everything and ran. Kitty ran the other way, into the house.

Things went okay at first. Skunks are good mousers. They are very clean. Unfortunately, they are largely nocturnal. They have claws and fangs just like a miniature grizzly, so it is a good thing they are friendly. Or they could be rabid. I am sure skunks have many other fine qualities as house pets, but it's just hard to think while you're having trouble breathing.

I thought Kitty would settle down like a regular cat if I just showed her enough love or ice cream. That worked like a charm at first. Looking back, I suppose that was just the honeymoon period. After a while, it was as if nothing was good enough. Before long, she wanted frozen yogurt, popcorn, and candy bars. I worried about what it did to her teeth, but I was just trying to avoid any more unpleasantness.

There is no good way to get a skunk out of your house. It's better not to let these smelly beasts inside in the first place. Once you are infested with skunk, all the I-told-you-so's in the world are not going to help. I tried to look on the positive side. No one was going to break into my house and rearrange my tackle box. Kitty was a good watchdog. Still I knew it was wrong to keep her penned up inside. There was nothing left to do but build a better skunk trap.

I built a ramp to the top of an antique milk barrel and baited it with ice cream, which would answer any questions about how I spent the weekend. When Kitty finally climbed into the skunk trap, she was really cranky and not the least bit shy about letting the world know it. Maybe it was the sugar buzz, because I think ice cream always made her cranky. There was nothing left to do but take her out into the forest to celebrate her newfound freedom.

Carrying her into the woods must have scared Kitty even more, to judge from the aroma. I set the milk can down in a mossy glen then went and got some air. I had to let Kitty out of the can.

I wanted to do this long distance. I hooked a big streamer fly to the edge of the milk can and backed away while letting the fly line out. I figured Kitty would be really upset when she got dumped out of the can. Sometimes it's best to get some distance from a strained relationship.

I must have stripped out about thirty yards of line and then I tightened the drag and set the hook. The milk can tipped over. Kitty took off like a shot and snagged up on the streamer fly. The drag on my reel screamed as the line melted into the tall grass. Kitty took off through the swamp like a greased monkey, peeling line until I felt a sickening snap and I knew I'd lost the skunk and my fly.

It was lonely after that. Kitty wouldn't come back no matter what kind of ice cream I had. Life goes on.

I got up early one morning in the dark to go fishing. I opened the door to a wave of aroma. A flood of emotions washed over me. Kitty was back, in the back of my boat, tangled in the landing net.

The reunion was bittersweet. She'd lost the Dungeness Special that was tangled in her tail, but she was going to be okay. Kitty had raised a real ruckus in the boat, tangling rods and dumping tackle boxes, giving a whole new meaning to the phrase *having a skunk in the boat*. As I shook her out of the landing net, Kitty sprayed me again for old time's sake, then waddled away to a new adventure.

The Spotted Owl

There are times I don't miss the good old days, until the statute of limitations expires. I'd hate to get caught impersonating an endangered species now. Back in the last century, it was a different story. It was a simpler time when loggers ruled the earth. The town of Forks had been declared the logging capital of the world. They planned to log the other planets later.

It seemed like a good idea at the time. By then we had logged our way across North America right to the edge of the continent. To the west lay the Pacific Ocean, a great treeless obstacle that stopped all logging. The end was in sight.

The first logging on the Olympic Peninsula was done by the Native Americans. Their material culture was based largely upon the western red cedar. Every part of the tree was used. The roots were used for baskets. The limbs were woven into ropes. The cedar bark was stripped from standing trees when the sap flowed in the spring and used for fiber. The cedar needles were medicine. The wood of the red cedar is light, aromatic, and resistant to rot. Cedar is easily split into boards.

About three thousand years ago, people started carving dugout canoes from a single cedar log using a drilling and burning process. The entire hull was then steamed into a graceful shape that was later copied by American clipper ships. Ocean-going canoes for whaling, war, or trading were said to carry up to seventy people.

About one thousand years ago, the first cedar plank houses appeared. The planks were split from cedar logs with elk-horn wedges and tied to a frame of cedar logs, then insulated with cattail mats. These shed-roof structures were called smoke houses. They could be over a hundred feet long, housing several families, each with their own hearth. The entrance to the smokehouse might be through a narrow opening at the base of a house pole, allowing only one person into the house at a time for added security in case of attack. Some house poles were fifty feet tall, carved with stylized representations of animals, fish, birds, supernatural spirits, and tribal crests that illustrated the heritage, status, and identity of the people living in the house.

Permanent villages were sometimes surrounded by palisades of upright logs a dozen feet high or more to guard against surprise attack.

Falling a large cedar with stone tools was a time-consuming process. One method involved chopping a small undercut into the cedar with an adze. A fire was started in the undercut and kept going until the tree burned through and fell over.

The first Europeans to discover the Olympic Peninsula began logging almost immediately in order to repair their ships. The British captain, John Meares, cut spars for his ship, *Felice*, in 1788. Captain George Vancouver cut spars for his ship, *Discovery*, in Discovery Bay in 1792. They would have cut the Douglas fir.

Sailors were natural loggers, experts at using blocks and rigging lines. Crews of sailors and hired Indians pulled the spars with ropes down trails made out of half-buried poles laid in the mud to form a puncheon road. With this kind of gear, it might have taken a week to move the log a hundred yards.

The first sawmill was built on the Olympic Peninsula at Port Ludlow in 1852. This was a water-powered mill that was lucky to cut two logs a day. By then, logging was done with oxen and draft horses.

In 1885, there was a new invention from down in Grays Harbor:

the donkey engine. This was a steam-powered winch that turned a drum filled with wire rope. The "donkey" was mounted to some log skids. Once it hooked up to a tail hold, it could skid itself through the woods to the spar tree. A special breed of loggers, the high climbers, would climb a prospective spar tree and cut the limbs on the way up. The top of the spar tree was cut off and rigged with the blocks and cables for dragging logs where no horse or ox could go.

Steam power allowed the mills to operate by burning their own waste. In 1887, the Puget Sound Cooperative Colony built a sawmill in Port Angeles that cut twenty thousand feet of lumber on a good day.

The real logging didn't start until the coming of the railroad. In 1914, Michael Earles built the largest sawmill in the world in Port Angeles. The Big Mill was a town all to itself, with a store, a cookhouse, and a three hundred–man bunkhouse. The "Big Mill" cut everything from shingles to beams 150 feet long from timber logged along the Strait of Juan de Fuca between the Elwha and Twin rivers.

During World War I, the Sitka spruce was valued for its strength and lightness in weight in the construction of airplanes. The Spruce Division, a paramilitary organization of ten thousand troops, was put to work logging spruce for the war effort. They built a spruce mill at the mouth of Ennis Creek in Port Angeles and a railroad around Lake Crescent to a tent camp at Lake Pleasant. The war ended before any spruce was logged. The railroad was used to haul logs from the Sol Duc, Calawah, and Dickey River logging operations to Port Angeles until 1954.

The trees of the Olympic Peninsula rainforest represent some of the largest and finest old-growth timber on the planet. World record specimens of fir, cedar, spruce, and hemlock can be found here. Early visitors to the rainforest described it as inexhaustible.

Darius Kinsey, a pioneer photographer who traveled around the logging camps, took a picture of a western red cedar as it was being cut down with axes and crosscut saws. The cedar was twenty-four feet in diameter. They might have had to weld two crosscut saws together to cut a tree that big. Crosscut saws were called misery whips for reasons that became apparent as soon as you pulled one.

If a cedar was hollow, one of the fallers might crawl inside to pull on the other end of the saw. Knowing just when to crawl out of the hollow tree you were cutting down would be crucial.

Those were the glory days of logging—six eleven-hour days a week with Sundays off to boil the lice out of your woolies and change the straw in your mattress. Logging camps were made up of narrow skid shacks that could be put on rail cars and moved to the next camp as the timber was cut.

They said that each logging camp had three crews: one quitting, one working, and one breaking in. It was a gypsy life style. They were called "gyppo loggers," these camps of freethinkers, shiftless bachelors, and married men trying to put together a grubstake to save the homestead.

The Olympic Peninsula rainforest has always been subject to fires and hurricanes. Quinault legends tell of a massive burn approximately three hundred years ago. That was long before there were any tourists to blame. The early pioneers used fire to clear land for farming. The pitchy roots of the Douglas fir could burn underground for weeks. Many a homesteader's fire got away from him. Back then, forest fires were seen as a good thing—clearing land for farming while opening up the view. Between 1885 and 1890, a series of runaway stump fires burned the northeastern foothills of the Olympics between Discovery Bay and Port Angeles.

In 1907, a forest fire started just west of Lake Crescent. Firefighters were sent with shovels, axes, and mattocks. The fire got away and burned Snider Ridge clear to Bear Creek on the Sol Duc River. This 12,000-acre burn became the Olympic Peninsula's first reforestation project. Unfortunately, once the trees were growing again, a cigarette tossed by a passing motorist on the newly constructed Olympic Loop Highway set the Sol Duc burn on fire again. For a while, it looked as if the Olympic Peninsula's inexhaustible forest would be burned before it could be logged.

In 1921, a hurricane hit Tatoosh Island with winds so strong it blew the lighthouse keeper's bull into the Strait of Juan de Fuca and hit the Peninsula, knocking down millions of board feet of timber. The trees were left to rot.

In September of 1951, a small fire on the railroad near Lake Crescent was fanned by a fifty-mile-an-hour east wind. The fire traveled eighteen miles in six hours and nearly incinerated the town of Forks.

By then, logging had evolved from the age of steam to diesel, with portable steel towers instead of spar trees. Fleets of log trucks replaced the railroads. Loggers salvaged the 30,000-acre Forks Burn for years, some days sending log trucks into Port Angeles at a rate of one per minute.

At this time, logging was typically done in a checkerboard pattern whereby alternate sections of timber were left unharvested. In October of 1962, another hurricane, the Columbus Day Storm, hit the Olympic Peninsula, knocking down millions of board feet of timber again. Loggers were able to salvage this blow down.

Meanwhile, Japan had rebuilt its economy following World War II. Japanese buyers began competing with each other for the Peninsula's fine old-growth timber.

The 1960s saw previously unharvested checkerboards that were clear-cut for the fast-developing Asian log market.

In the 1970s, the cut increased. Entire watersheds were cut right up to the Olympic National Park boundary. The timber was stored and sorted in massive yards, and then shipped to Japan as raw logs.

Not many people had ever heard of a spotted owl. As kids growing up in the woods, we'd seen great horned owls, barn owls, and even great gray owls, but you hardly ever saw a spotted owl. They have always been rare.

In 1990, the spotted owl was declared threatened by the logging of old-growth timber. Loggers were shut down all across the Pacific Northwest. It was hard times for the working man. Emotions ran high. Jobs were scarce.

I saw an ad in a newspaper for the Spotted Owl Survey School. I thought surveying owls would be easy. I was wrong.

Nothing prepared me for that first day at Spotted Owl Survey School. We were herded into a concrete barn. An instructor in a game warden suit told us to forget everything we knew about bird watching. We were told to look to our left and look to our right, because two out of three of us were going to wash out before hell-week was over.

He put us through an exhaustive series of owl identification drills that eliminated a third of the class. Their bird-watching careers over before they began. Our bird-watching marathon was just beginning.

We were forced to mimic a series of owl calls while the instructor paced the room whacking his leather boot with a riding crop. Then we were herded into a drafty bus that drove us up a logging road. After a bumpy ride, the bus skidded to a stop on top of a narrow ridge above a vast forest. It was a second-growth forest, meaning it had already been logged. I thought it was funny to be looking for spotted owls in a second-growth forest, but that was the only place I'd ever seen them.

We were supposed to learn field tactics. Spotted owls are called during their mating season when we are all at our most vulnerable. When the spotted owl calls, they have revealed their presence to other owls—the great horned and the barred owl. These larger owls eat spotted owls.

I asked a stupid question, "Doesn't surveying the spotted owls endanger them?" That ended my spotted owl survey career. I vowed never to use my knowledge for evil.

The old-growth timber was saved from the loggers. Any bug-infested, blown-down or burned-out old growth was no longer open for salvage. It was left for the spotted owl. The surviving loggers had to cut smaller and smaller trees, which they did with larger and larger machines.

By the 1990s, a logger with a feller-buncher machine could harvest five acres of second-growth timber a day, untouched by human hands. They began logging the forest like there was no tomorrow. Not that I cared. The clear cuts grew blackberries, deer, elk, and firewood as far as I was concerned.

Meanwhile, the numbers of spotted owls continued to decline in the remaining old growth. Biologists determined the barred owl, which is believed to have arrived from Canada, was causing the spotted owl to spiral down the rat hole to extinction.

I was seriously disturbed. For years, we had been told the Canadian owls only ate mice the American owls didn't want. We believed Canadian owls would only inhabit nest sites too dilapidated for an American owl. Until it was too late and we heard horror stories of the spotted owl mating season being overwhelmed by barred owls in a manner too shocking for a family newspaper.

The owl biologists blamed the usual list of suspects for the spotted owl's decline: loggers, the weather, and the barred owl. Typically, they somehow failed to mention themselves in the list of owl predators. For while one group of dedicated biologists was busy sabotaging the spotted owl breeding season with a rash of phony calls, another bunch of dedicated biologists was busy reintroducing the spotted owl's worst nightmare back to the Olympic Peninsula: the fisher.

Fishers are large, ferocious, tree-climbing members of the weasel family that specialize in finding the eggs and young of the spotted owl in an old-growth forest. With biologist friends like that, the spotted owl didn't need any more predators. The biologists proposed a final solution—shooting the barred owls.

Once again, I couldn't have cared less. I figured the barred owl had it coming, being an illegal alien and all. But still, I thought shooting was a little drastic. America had to do something, but I thought they should call the border patrol to deport the Canadian birds before the mystic hooting of an American owl in our wilderness was replaced with "eh." I thought at the time if the barred owl didn't straighten up and fly, right we'd turn it over to another government agency with a long history of making birds, fish, and game disappear, the Washington State Department of Fish and Wildlife.

Then one evening, my peaceful world was shattered by an incoming spotted-owl call. Without thinking, I called back. My call was answered by another and then another call. It was too late when I realized those weren't owls at all. They were spotted owl surveyors. I was being triangulated. It had been years since I had called an owl. It's a use-it-or-lose-it thing. What if I accidentally answered with a barred owl call? That's when I really wished I hadn't slept through half of my days in owl school. I could have been impersonating either an endangered species or vermin with a price on its head. Either way, there was a SWAT team of rabid biologists headed my way with blood in their eye. I put on my walking shoes and started up the ridge, hooting like a flock of owls in heat.

Barred owl, spotted owl, it didn't matter what kind of owl I was by then. There was a team of biologists hot on my trail, no doubt convinced they were about to bust some sort of owl orgy that broke all rules of animal behavior.

It was pitch dark when I climbed out of the canyon. I staggered onto a logging road and into the headlights of a truckload of loggers. I waved them down and explained how the biologists were after me. I jumped into the back of the truck as it tore off down that logging road as if the devil himself was chasing it.

There are few men more courageous than loggers. They face death and dismemberment every day. One mention of the biologists, however, had the loggers terrified. They were convinced that once the biologists eliminated the barred owl, the loggers would be next.

The biologists would have to find their way back to their vehicle first, out of the maze of canyons they had been lured into with their own bloodlust. I quit calling owls after that.

After a while, the surveyors went away. They left scads of plastic ribbons with funny writing on them through acres of forest. It made good fire starter in a pinch. But like I said, it was a long time ago. I don't call owls anymore.

The Love Birds

Then it was summer. The hot sun melted the winter's snow from the Olympic Mountains. The Dungeness River grew into a raging, chocolate-colored torrent that was in danger of flooding the lowlands. You never ran out of worry on the homestead. After the flood, the woods were tinder dry. One little spark could turn the neighborhood into a fiery holocaust.

Summer brought another threat to the homestead that was worse than all the floods and forest fires put together: tourists.

I'll never forget the last time a van of tourists showed up at my homestead. The doors opened and the tourists burst out like a SWAT team, all asking the same question, "Where's the bathroom?"

I knew from hard experience this rush on the bathroom would lead to another flood—the flooding of the septic system.

After I pumped out the bathroom, the tourist demands became more insistent. They wanted to go clamming and fishing.

I asked the tourists how they would like it if I came over to their big city to rob the liquor store.

"That's illegal," the tourists said.

"So is clamming and fishing," I explained. The clams are polluted and the fish are endangered. Clamming and fishing are federal crimes here. You'd probably get off with a lighter sentence robbing the liquor store back home.

The locals had to come up with creative new ways of milking the tourists' dollars beyond clamming and fishing.

I gave the tourists tennis rackets and led them to the vegetable garden. I was growing a special arctic corn that might make it ankle high by the Fourth of July. There were the skeletal remains of a potato crop being devoured by a plague of slugs.

"Go for distance," I said, explaining the finer points of slug tennis. We had a volley in no time, until the rackets clogged up. And I really should have insisted on eye protection.

Then it was off to the woods for a real old-fashioned firewood ride. That's like a hayride, only instead of sitting on some moldy old mound of hay on a clunky wagon, you're styling on a pile of firewood in the back of a speeding truck.

First, we had to get the truck started. That meant we had to push the truck. This required teamwork, agility, and brute strength, which made it an ideal tourist activity.

Once we got the truck started, we had the firewood ride dreams are made of. That's what tourist season meant to me—making memories that would last a lifetime. We unloaded the firewood. I got the bleeding stopped. The tourists continued yammering about the bathroom. I explained how we'd have to snake the septic tank first. Unfortunately, there's just never enough time on a vacation. I knew I would miss them, but they had to leave first, before any more tourists showed up.

I had just settled into the solitude of silence when some more guests dropped in. They were honeymooners from Canada. Vacation guests from hell. You know the type. Messy and loud, they came by for a visit and would not leave. I called them the "love birds."

She was "in the family way," which must have been her excuse for sitting around staring blankly into space for hours on end. He was one of those "needy" guys, who wouldn't let his mate eat without watching over her; he was totally worthless.

They'd stand around for hours on end making enough love talk to keep a soap opera in heat. It was embarrassing to watch. I felt like

I was in the way. I was only trying to help. That's why I became an unlicensed relationship counselor—to write about the relationship problems of others in a non-judgmental way.

He was a large, overweight male with an obsessive-compulsive delusion that I had personal feelings toward his significant other. She was a petite, dusky temptress with perfect posture who, judging from the endless hours spent preening, cared for little other than her looks.

I couldn't have a word with her without him getting in the way and making an ugly scene. Things came to a head one morning. I was serving scones and jam al fresco by the pond. All of the sudden, it was as if he wasn't hungry, so no one else could eat. I told him he could go on a diet if he wanted to, but the rest of us were having our brunch.

Frankly, that's when she started showing a sudden interest in me. Maybe she just wanted a scone, but she waddled over to me like I was her big daddy.

Then things got physical. She appeared mildly amused with precipitating an ugly scene. He grabbed the edge of my bathrobe in his beak and began shaking it like a wet rag.

Did I mention these lovebirds were Canada geese? Sure, they sound great on an autumn night, way up high in a perfect V, flying to somewhere else far away. Try living with them. The only thing worse than having Canada geese at your house is to have a family of them.

If the constant honking of the nesting geese from dawn till dark doesn't drive you over the brink, the disgusting carpet of droppings these birds produce will. Once the goslings appear, the geese will attack almost anything to defend their brood or demand another scone.

No problem is too large to run away from. It would be summer soon, after all; a perfect time for me to go on vacation.

1 *Honeybee on Dandelion*

2 *Male Blue Grouse*

3 *Female Blue Grouse*

4 *Canada Goose*

5 Firewood

6 *Shadow*

7 Flossie

8 Chantrelles

9 Stone Tool

10 *Plow Blade*

11 *The Sequim Prairie*

12 *Bucky and Entourage*

13 *Bucky the Elk Memorial*

The Deer Fence

Springtime always gave me hope that the garden would grow better this year than last. My goal was a garden where I could harvest something the year round. It sounded simple enough—to live off the land—but there were a lot of factors working against the success of a wilderness garden.

I planted early and often. The rows sprouted with industrial precision. Just as the tiny plants broke through the surface, a biblical infestation of squirrels, chipmunks, and kangaroo mice swept through the garden like a plague. They seemed to prefer the sprouted seed of beans, corn, and peas to a boring diet of fir cones. So it was a kind of lucky break for the garden when the squirrels and chipmunks decided to move into the house.

Once inside, these playful creatures found a whole new world of things to play with … like tennis balls. I had no idea squirrels liked to play tennis at all hours. Then a pair of wildcats showed up. Crabbait and Wadcutter cleaned out the garden pests in no time. And then it was really too bad when the kitties got eaten by coyotes.

By midsummer, the garden blossomed into a massive field of food. Until the deer found it. The deer ate the garden down to the roots and then dug the roots out and ate them too. I have heard many theories from experts about how to keep deer out of the garden. I must have tried them all.

At first, I thought it was a simple matter of hunting the deer. Every fall the hills were crawling with hunters. I thought all those nimrods would put a lead fence around the garden. That didn't work.

It turns out deer hunters have more excuses than fishermen. Opening day of deer season was too dry. There was no point in walking around looking for deer, the hunters said. You'd make too much noise trying to sneak up on deer in the dry brush. The moon was out. That was always bad for hunting. The deer went completely nocturnal.

Then it started raining and blowing. It was storming so hard there was no way you could see a deer. You'd have to be nuts to be out in the woods with the branches flying and the trees falling over.

The deer hunters all claimed what they really needed was some tracking snow. Until then, there was nothing they could do but ride around and sight in their guns.

The amount of ammunition consumed in this process was amazing. Roads were paved with empty brass. By hunting season, the deer had been shell-shocked by months of constant gunfire.

A deer would have to be stuck in a sensory deprivation chamber not to know it was hunting season. Many deer left the woods and moved to town for the duration.

Truth is, even if the deer hunters could have shot a deer, it would not have saved the garden. The hunters could only shoot bucks, which left more of the garden for the does, who acted like they'd been done a favor.

The snow the deer hunters were waiting for did not come until after the end of hunting season. This triggered a migration of still more deer from the mountains. They were hungry and had taught the rest of the deer how to dig carrots. I would have to build a deer fence if I was ever going to have a garden.

I heard if you strung fishing line around your garden, the deer would walk into the line, get spooked, and never bother the garden again. That sounded good. I had enough fishing line to stretch to the moon and back. I strung some line around the garden and was pleasantly surprised to find that it worked—until after sunset, when the deer walked right through the fishing line.

I heard if you tied some sacks to the fishing line, they'd make a rustling sound that would frighten the deer. I must have been desperate to believe that one. The deer spend their lives hunted by cougars, bears, coyotes, bobcats, packs of domestic dogs, and the worst predator of them all, man. How could a creature that survives all these vicious predators be scared of a plastic sack? They're not.

I heard if you put some human or dog hair in the sack, the deer would smell it and be scared away. No.

Maybe the fishing-line-and-sack deer fence would have worked if I'd put some hand grenades in the sacks. Eventually something big got tangled up in the fishing line fence and walked off trailing the whole mess into the swamp.

There was nothing left to do but build a real fence: posts with wire in between. It was to be a monument eight feet tall that the deer could not jump over. The fence was going to be so big I could make the garden bigger. I cut some cedar fence posts and set to work, digging holes.

I'll never forget the morning of the groundbreaking. The chore could be postponed no more. It wasn't raining, too cold, or too hot and there were no witnesses or excuses. I cut through the thick sod with a shovel. It looked like easy digging for a while. Then I hit a chunk of metal. It was a thin chunk of steel. I thought I could move the fence. I could make the garden just a little smaller. I dug another hole and thumped into another chunk of steel. Another hole found more metal.

Feeling cursed, I dug for another hour before figuring out what I was up against. It was a windmill, brought here by the homesteaders who had settled these hills. This must have been a prosperous farm to have a windmill. Most of the homesteaders had to pack their water from the well or spring or creek. You wonder what sort of calamity hit the farm, leaving the windmill under a layer of burnt earth. It took the rest of the day to uncover the buried windmill. That made eight hours of digging, without one fencepost sunk.

The next day started like the day before. I started digging a posthole ten feet away from the windmill and hit another chunk of metal. It was part of a cast-iron woodstove. It might have been all that was left of a pioneer house after a fire.

I began to dig another hole. There, just beneath the sod, lay the iron blade of a plow.

I kept digging.

I found a rusted chunk of inch-and-a-half-diameter braided wire rope in the next hole—the big rigging the loggers used to log the big timber out of the burn. The garden must have been the landing for a high-lead logging show. They used a donkey engine and a spar tree to yard logs out of the canyon. A nearby stump bore the marks of the springboard the loggers used to climb the tree when they cut it down. The stump must have been a tail-hold for the spar tree, from the way it was still lashed up with rusty cable and railroad spikes.

I kept digging holes in a line sloping down to the pond. Every fence posthole seemed to uncover a new treasure. I found an axe head, a wagon wheel rim, and some strange rocks that appeared to be fractured in half. They might have been cooking rocks.

Native Americans wove baskets that could hold water. They put hot rocks in the water to boil their food. Some of the rocks would shatter, leaving signs of a camp. I found other rocks that seemed to have been worked into scrapers that would fit right in the palm of your hand. I noticed something white. It was a piece of chert that had been flaked off on both sides.

Here was the work of a craftsman, dead for thousands of years. The man who chipped the flakes off this stone might have been from a tribe of mastodon hunters who came into the country some fourteen thousand years ago. Even a small mastodon could feed a large family for weeks before they threw the bones into the waterhole and moved on. There was no telling what remains lay in the peat at the bottom of the pond.

It would lie there a while longer. I still had some postholes to dig. Then I had to sink the posts, stretch some wire, and make a gate.

I finished the deer fence and stood back to look. Thousands of years of humanity's labor lay buried beneath my feet. I thought of how the mammoth hunters, the Indians, the homesteaders, and the loggers all left a mark and passed on. We walked the same ground and looked at the same hills at the end of the day. We shared a kinship with the land. The haunted valley wasn't lonely any more.

It was only a matter of time before my deer fence would rot and rust into the swamp along with the efforts of my predecessors, to be buried under piles of sediment. Until someone dug it up.

Meanwhile I had my deer fence. The deer fence saved the garden until they figured out how to open the gate.

Blackberry Heaven

I thought I had died and gone to blackberry heaven. It had to be the hottest day of summer, a time to head for the hills to gather free food no matter what it cost. Scattered through the forest was a banquet of berries, and I was going to pick them all.

The salmon berries were in their final stage of perfection. Their colors changed from the orange flesh of salmon to a burgundy shade of red. Gorging on salmon berries, I stumbled into an old river channel and found that rarest of all wild berries, the wild strawberry. They grew in a mat on a carpet of moss.

The Seneca considered the wild strawberry sacred. The earliest strawberries of the season were thought to have medicinal value, impart wisdom, and affect dreams. Strawberries were said to grow along the road to heaven. Some said there is a spring in heaven that issues strawberry juice.

All I know for sure is a good patch of wild strawberries is a little piece of heaven right here on earth. I fed my way across the strawberry patch to a rotten fir stump. Growing out of the stump was a magnificent bush covered with red huckleberries.

Picking huckleberries is slow work. The Indians combed the huckleberries off the bushes into blankets. I just broke off some branches; I could pick the berries off later.

If the red huckleberries were ripe, it could only mean one thing. The blue huckleberries were just coming on. What I saw next made me drop my huckleberries.

It was a towering thorny cane covered with blackcaps. I ate my fill and moved on. Now I was looking for blackberries, the little wild ones that grow in secret patches, the further from the road the better.

Picking blackberries is an extremely competitive sport. You must find the berries before the bears get them.

The bears have every advantage in the berry patch. They can pick at night, filling a paunch that can hold gallons of berries that could have been your pie.

Blackberries grow on thorny vines amid thorny bushes. A blackberry picker's hands can look like they got mauled by a bear. You can't let the bears scare you out of a good berry patch. There are worse things.

I worked my way into the middle of an old clear cut that was grown up enough to be miserable walking. The logging slash, limbs, and broken tree tops were just rotten enough to break once you stepped on them. Blackberries like to grow in old logging shows, so if you find a good patch, chances are you can thank a logger.

I stepped up on a log. It buckled, sending me forward into a small, excavated bunker left when a big tree fell over. There I stood, waist deep in rotten branches with my foot caught in a mountain beaver hole.

I was surrounded by heavy vines with skeins of shiny black berries. Some ripened in full sun. Others were shaded by the sword ferns. Each berry had a slightly different flavor that was more than the sum of its parts.

On a good day in most parts, you could pick a gallon of blackberries. This was a berry patch where five gallons were possible. And it was only the first picking. The berries would continue for weeks. I was rich beyond my wildest dreams.

Blackberries have always been valuable. The Indians owned berry patches. They dried blackberries into cakes. In pioneer times, blackberries might be the only fruit you had. Blackberry picking was a tradition where your social standing in the community could be determined by the gallons of blackberries you picked.

Reputations could be tarnished with foul accusations that you put blackcaps in with the blackberries to increase your gallon count or spied on another picker's patch and sicced the dogs on him. It's like we say in the berry patch, "You don't fill your bucket without smashing a few berries."

I thought of all the miles and years of searching through the brush and canyons of the cutover lands to find this at last—the best blackberry patch I ever saw. Berries don't pick themselves. I got to work and clawed handfuls of them into my bucket.

There was a moment of berry-picking bliss. Then the sensation of a hundred red-hot needles caught my attention.

Bees!

Bald-faced hornets! It is a curious fact that the best blackberry patches seem to grow on top of hornets nests. Experts advise you to remain calm when you are attacked by hornets. These same people will tell you to remain calm when you are lost or sinking. I was calm until I got stung by the hornets. Then I took off out of that berry patch like I was on fire. I made it out to an old road. I took off my hat to swat a hornet and got hit in the side of the head by another one.

I'd lost my bucket and one of my shoes, but no matter. I had found blackberry heaven and I was going back.

Raccoons

I'll have to admit when I first saw the baby raccoons curled up in the middle of the road, my first impulse was to run over them. Because if there is one creature on this earth I can't stand, it is the raccoon. If you ever went out to check your chicken house and found what was left of your pet laying-hens after the raccoons ate them alive, or saw an orchard or a corn patch that's been clear cut by a coon party, you'd understand.

Things could be worse.

You'd know that, if raccoons ever came down your chimney. Then there were the loggers who lured the raccoons into their cabin after they'd been drinking beer, the raccoons that is. Raccoons were made for wide-open spaces and tend to run amuck when trapped indoors for any length of time.

I wanted no part of any raccoons, baby or not. I drove right on by and left them. Still, I thought I should check on them later, and sure enough, the poor baby raccoons hadn't moved. They were getting cooked in the middle of the gravel road. They might have been dehydrated.

A raven flew over and gave a lone croak, probably just waiting for someone to run the coons over and tenderize them for a noonday meal. What could I do? What would you do?

Then I saw two ravens circling. I moved the baby raccoons out of the middle of the road to a hollow cedar stump. The three of them stayed rolled up in a little ball. I went away thinking I'd done the best thing you can do for baby wild animals; now ignore them, they'll go away.

It's illegal, bad, and wrong to mess with baby wild animals. I wouldn't recommend it to anyone. Still, I couldn't just let the little fellows curl up and starve after their mother hadn't come back to get them the next day. I poured some milk into a glove and breakfast was served. They ate like starving wolverines. This was very messy, but they groomed each other clean in no time.

After a few days in the cedar stump, it was clear the mother raccoon was not coming back. There seemed to be a lot of raccoons around, more than I'd seen in years, but these poor little coons' mother was not one of them.

I thought it was up to me to find the baby raccoons a new home. I took them into town in a box marked "Kittens $5." They didn't find a new home, but it's a great way to clear out a Laundromat.

By then, I had built an emotional bond. They had adjusted to solids—chicken-flavored cat food. We spent a lot of time together grooming, feeding, and bonding. I tried to train the raccoons by enrolling them in a dog obedience class. I thought with those little hands, they could be a lot of help. They could make good seeing-eye coons. That didn't work out.

One day at the feed store in town, I was talking to a flatlander from down in the valley. Somehow, the subject of raccoons came up. The old guy went off. When he began talking about raccoons, his fists were clenched, his face went red. He became so angry he started spitting, so we had a lot in common when it came to raccoons. It turned out he was a retiree who lived on a golf course. The raccoons had made a stinking mess of the golf course. So he live-trapped a bunch of them using chicken for bait and dumped the delinquent raccoons up in the woods right next to my chicken house.

It all made sense now. But it was too late. All my hens had been eaten. It was time for a little payback. I began teaching the baby raccoons how to retrieve golf balls. I started live-trapping moles.

That's when things got ugly, but like I said, by now I was out for revenge. I began collecting slugs from the endless supply in my garden. I kept them in a five-gallon bucket with a layer of fresh greens.

By the end of summer, the raccoons were shagging golf balls like Labrador retrievers. I had a six-pack of live moles ready to dig in and a five-gallon bucket of slugs. I drove into the flatlands with blood in my eye. I dropped the raccoons off in the lobby of the clubhouse to create a diversion while I sprinkled the moles and slugs out on the fairway.

It was good to be alive.

Firewood

I enjoy few things more than cutting firewood. The smell of fresh sawdust and the ringing of the iron wedge as it's pounded into a round wheel of wood takes me back to an earlier time, when the earth was wood powered. Whoever said cutting firewood warms you twice, once in the cutting and once in the burning, was a real greenhorn. Cutting firewood warms you in more ways than you can shake a stick at. There's nothing like jerking a pull cord on a chainsaw that won't start, to warm you up. After five or ten minutes, you may want to check for fuel. Got gas? Then you have to get creative. Take out the spark plug and give it a few pulls. Put the spark plug back in. Continue pulling. Drag the saw back to the road. Tangle it in a mess of blackberry vines. Step into the mountain beaver hole and go down in a pile of limbs and nettles. You should be plenty warm by then.

Cutting firewood in the summer might not seem like a good idea, and it isn't. It's best to cut wood in the spring so that it cures all summer and is dry for winter. Burning green or wet wood in your stove allows flammable tar to build up in your chimney.

Chimney fires can be a great way to take the chill out of a cold winter morning or an embarrassing way to burn your house down. This can all be avoided by cleaning your chimney and burning dry wood.

I did the cooking on a wood stove at the homestead. Nothing but the finest stove wood is required if you plan on boiling water on a cook stove, I used cedar for kindling, fir limbs to get a steady blaze, and then topped it off with a big chunk of old-growth fir bark.

Bark was a valuable commodity there.

Let's say you were too shiftless and lazy to cut any wood for the winter. Dry bark could be found year round if you knew where to look. You wanted to find a standing dead tree. Loggers called them widow makers for obvious reasons. The old snags could be so rotten they shook like a tower of Jell-O.

My old stump-rancher friends used to peel the bark off widow makers. Those were the good old days when children were allowed to play with dynamite. They'd put on Dad's climbing spurs and climb up a likely widow maker, setting charges in the bark. Then, lighting the fuse on the way down, they'd run a ways off and watch the fun.

I used to peel the bark off widow makers with a long pole that was sharpened on one end. That was dangerous enough, as slabs of bark weighing hundreds of pounds would break loose from the tree and fly in all directions. It was all worthwhile though when it came to keeping the cook stove going.

Falling a widow-maker is a good example of the woodpile theory of relativity. A standing widow maker can appear to grow larger as you approach it, so that by the time you've made the undercut, it looks like a truckload of wood. Once upon the ground, the log doesn't look quite as big as it did while it was falling over. It can look like about a half a truckload. Once you start sawing it into lengths and splitting it into pieces, you're sure you've got more than a truckload. Loading the truck dispels this myth. Your average firewood cutter is invariably a few chunks shy of a load. A truckload of wood makes a massive pile on the ground after you throw it out of the truck and then shrinks again as you load it into the woodshed with more wood than you could ever dream of burning. The load then appears to shrink still smaller with the passing of winter until you realize you should have cut more wood. Meanwhile, each piece of firewood has been handled, fondled, and moved enough times to develop an emotional relationship with it.

Cutting wood became an obsession. I wanted a woodpile large enough to be seen from space. At the time, I didn't care where it came from.

Windfalls also make good firewood. After the storms of winter, I'd cruise the woods looking for trees that were blown over. You'd think windfalls would be easier to cut into firewood because they are already on the ground, but they are not. Windfalls are especially dangerous where two or more fall together in a heap. The tremendous pressure of the downed logs pressing against each other can be released with the slightest touch of a sharp saw.

The logs can literally pop loose in all directions as the pressure is released when you least expect it. I should know. I got nailed by a windfall. It exploded from a tangle and landed on my leg. I was trapped like a rat in a trap.

The experience gave a whole new meaning to the word tree-hugger. I remembered the number one rule of safety while working in the woods: never work alone. I sensed movement. A raven was gliding through the forest. It landed on a limb not ten feet away. I thought I knew that raven. I had talked to him and fed him for years. It wasn't until that moment that I understood what he was.

I looked him in the eye and knew how it felt to die. I reached for my chainsaw. It started with the first pull. I cut the log off my leg and dragged myself back home. I don't talk to ravens anymore.

Fall Chores

Autumn was my favorite season in the Olympic Mountains. The evening sun painted the hills a dark shade of purple. The leaves turned a riot of red, yellow, and orange. After the first dusting of snow, the mountains seemed close enough to touch in the crisp clear air. Then there was an early flight of teal, and a chill in the mornings you could not ignore. It was time to shift into high gear and get the fall chores done before the storms of winter.

Digging potatoes had to be my favorite fall chore on the homestead. It was the payoff for the summer's work and the secure feeling that no matter how bad the coming winter got, at least I had a potato.

A member of the nightshade family, potatoes were cultivated in South America twenty-five hundred years before Christ. The Spanish conquistadors invaded South America looking for gold, but they also found the potato.

Those were the good old days when all you had to do to own land was to plant a cross, claim you owned it, and you did. When Balboa first sighted the Pacific Ocean in 1513, he took possession of it and all the lands on its shores for the Spanish crown of Castile.

In 1521, Cortez whipped the Aztecs of Mexico. In 1531, Pizarro beat the Incas of Peru. The conquistador act did not play well on the Olympic Peninsula.

Captain Bruno Heceta of the Santiago made the first landfall by a European in what is now Washington State, on Destruction Island, July 14, 1775. Things went okay at first, but then, no one was at home at the time.

It didn't go so well for his partner, Captain Quadra of the Sonora. He sent a longboat crew to shore for water, south of the Hoh river. The Indians, unaware they were Spanish subjects, massacred the longboat crew in the surf as soon as they landed.

In 1792, Spanish built a fort at Neah Bay. Called Nunez Gaona, it was said to include some Peruvian Indians, so we can assume they brought the first potatoes to the Olympic Peninsula.

Nunez Gaona only lasted a few months. That was how long it took the Spanish to figure out there was no gold in these hills. The only other treasure was the sea otter. They would soon be hunted to extinction, so there was no point in hanging around.

The potatoes remained.

The potato became an important crop to the Indians, replacing the camass bulb. Within a few years, potato cultivation spread south to the Ozette and Quileute and Hoh rivers and then east to the Dungeness where they were planted on every available patch of open ground. Potatoes were one of the chief crops of the stump ranchers. These were the people who tried to farm the land the loggers had left behind. Pulling the stumps was a luxury not many could afford, so the stump ranchers planted where they could. That first harvest was a bumper crop. Declining yields grew smaller spuds as the thin forest soil was played out and went to use as a hay meadow or returned to forest.

I knew some of the old-time stump ranchers. I traded them for seed potatoes of every variety of Olympic Peninsula potato I could find, and then planted them in a layer of native peat moss and stood back. By midsummer, some vines were eight feet long. By autumn, I had the strangest crop of potatoes anywhere. They were red and white, and blue and yellow, all just waiting to be dug.

Still, they could wait a while longer. As long as the potatoes were covered with enough soil, they would be perfectly fine all winter, even if I had to paw my way through a couple of feet of snow to get at them. So there was no point in digging them ahead of time. Another problem solved.

Picking apples was another favorite fall chore. The Olympic Peninsula is blessed with an abundance of pioneer homestead orchards. Different varieties of these heritage apples ripen from August through December.

It's easy to spot these relics of an earlier, simpler time. Pioneer fruit trees can grow fifty feet tall and as big around. Climbing one of these monstrosities is risky. How you get the apples onto the ground without bruising them is anyone's guess. Sure, you can climb a ladder to pick apples, if you have a death wish.

It seemed ridiculous that anyone would pick apples by hand anyway. There were many other more convenient harvest options available to the homesteader. By blasting the limbs off the apple trees with a shotgun (12-gauge or larger), you could do your fall pruning while you got your apples picked.

That's why it's so tragic to run out of shotgun shells when it's apple-knocking time. So I guess it's really okay that the bears got into the orchard and ran amuck.

The bears had it all figured. They waited until I was out of shotgun shells and the apples had reached their ripest perfection to skulk into the orchard just before dark.

They climbed up in the trees and out on a limb where the best fruit grows. There was the sound of breaking wood in the night. Morning found the trees bedraggled, stripped of fruit and leaves, with nothing much left to prune or pick.

There were still plenty of chores to keep me busy. After spending the summer curing in the sun, this year's crop of firewood was ready to be put under cover. My enjoyment of stacking firewood is right up there with cutting it.

Woodpile management is an art and a science rolled into one. Stacking firewood is not something you want to rush into, not while the country is alive with a summer's hatch of bald-faced hornets and yellow jackets.

It's bad enough just walking through the brush. Just knock over a hornets nest in your woodpile for a nature experience you'll never forget. I always thought it was best to wait for a freeze to kill the bees before you pawed through the firewood.

That's life on the homestead. We moved with the rhythm of the seasons. The summer sun grew the garden. The fall rains brought the salmon. By then, it was a time to go fishing, so any chore that went undone was liable to stay that way.

Shadow

Of the many dangerous beasts inhabiting the Olympic Peninsula wilderness, the pet-dumpers are the worst. These are people for whom the responsibility of pet ownership is just too much. They routinely solve the problem by simply dropping the family pet off up a dirt road somewhere. It is a cruel fate for a poor dog or cat to be left in the woods.

After thousands of years of domestication, these poor creatures are forced into a world with no place for them. The lucky ones enter the food chain immediately. They are killed and eaten by predators that belong in the woods. The rest of these disposable pets wander around hungry, afraid, and abandoned.

They are instinctively drawn to human company, and yet they remember what humans did to them. These starving, half-wild animals can be scary. You're liable to meet them raiding the garbage can.

That's how I met Shadow. He was a black cat, the spitting image of a miniature black panther. I spooked him out of a garbage can where he exploded like a streak of hot tar. At the time, I needed a cat like a hole in the head, but I couldn't just watch him starve.

I left a bowl of milk out for him. The next morning the milk was gone. The cat was still hiding, but I had made a friend. I kept leaving milk out and he kept drinking it. Every once in a while, I would surprise him sleeping in a woodpile or a shed. He always ran away.

Over a period of weeks, I kept moving the milk closer to the back door of the house. After a while, I could talk to the cat and he wouldn't run away.

I bought some real cat food. We sat in the sun while he ate. Then the strangest thing happened. One morning there was a half-eaten baby rabbit lying by the back door. Shadow was bringing home the bacon. I had been adopted. This had disturbing implications. I was about to find out what an awesome predator the domestic house cat can be.

Every morning there was one, two, or sometimes three dead animals lying by the door with large chunks eaten out of them. A weasel, a vole, a mole, a shafted flicker, and then, a baby grouse.

That was the final straw. I was planning on eating the grouse myself once they grew up and hunting season was open.

There was only one thing to do. I had to get rid of Shadow before he started taking on the big game. He was such a vicious predator it wouldn't have surprised me to see a dead fawn on the lawn. I decided to dump the cat in town.

It's not as cruel as it sounds. He had a garage, regular grub, and a vet. He grew some gray hairs and a big belly. The last time I saw him, he was lying in the sun. A family of quail was scolding him. Shadow did not even look up. He was retired.

On the way back to the homestead, I noticed someone had dumped a couch along the road. There on the couch was another abandoned cat, waiting.

Since then, I have proposed a spay-neuter program for pet-dumpers. I think it's the least we can do.

Flossie

I suppose you could say I was a connoisseur of compost. I had spent years creating a composting dynamo that would completely dissolve a fish head in less than a month. It's like the old saying: if you build a better composter, something will beat a path to your door. It did. I was up early that morning, checking to see if the compost was still steaming.

Something beat a path to the door of the composter. A salvaged hundred-pound section of heavy steel rock-screen had been torn out of the way. My beloved composter was ruined. Offal and half-rotted fish heads were scattered across the garden like so much garbage.

I rebuilt my composting dynamo and sat back to watch for saboteurs.

I saw her one evening, strolling along the edge of the swamp. She was built like a brick smokehouse, an enchanting creature with beautiful jet-black hair. She started hanging around. I knew my composting days were numbered.

I remember the good times. Eating, wallowing, and eating. There's a period of adjustment in any relationship. She used to go on eating binges. Maybe it's my fault, but I couldn't bring myself to say anything. Like the time she ate an orchard full of apples. It must have upset her tummy judging from the mess in the yard.

People started talking and asking silly questions like, "Why doesn't she do that in the woods like all the other bears?"

They mentioned shooting the bear for a bear rug. I thought Flossie needed that bear hide more than my fancy friends did.

I wondered how the city folks would like it if I pulled up in their driveway and started shooting their pets. They'd probably have me arrested.

Flossie didn't like to be shot, even with a camera. I took her picture while she was climbing a tree. She growled at the flash and came down the tree clacking her jaws.

It was a bad time to run out of fish heads. She overreacted by eating an entire hornet's nest in one sitting. That made her cranky. I blamed myself, but couldn't help wondering if she didn't just like me for my compost.

Things went a little crazy after that. I mentioned the extra weight she was putting on for hibernation. I meant it in the nicest possible way. I had no idea it was a cruel and hurtful remark.

The compost was soured. Flossie stayed away for days on end. I heard from some flatlanders that she'd been on their porch eating fruit. They scared her away with loud noises. They said they were looking for a permanent solution.

I told them that loud noises scared Flossie. She preferred Mozart. As for a permanent solution, if she wanted to hibernate at their fancy house with the automatic this and electric that, I would not stand in the way of her happiness.

Life goes on. I built a new composter. So far, nothing has bothered it.

The Golden Harvest

I always looked forward to the rains of autumn. That's what made the mushrooms sprout. Then it was time to head for the hills and the secret patches of the golden chanterelle.

I've heard it said there are over five hundred varieties of mushrooms on the Olympic Peninsula. Many are said to be edible. A friend once said he'd eaten over fifty different species of mushrooms. I'd drop by for supper and eat many of these mushrooms just to be polite. Some of them were very good. Others tasted like boot leather or moldy sawdust. They seemed to grow larger as I chewed. My friend was always asking how I felt after supper and holding up five fingers for me to count.

You want to be very careful when it comes to identifying wild mushrooms. Not everyone who says they are a mushroom expert actually is one. Read a mushroom ID book. Take a mushroom class. Stay away from mushrooms with names like destroying angel, slippery Jack, or panther amanita. Symptoms of mushroom poisoning include vomiting, seizures, and death. There are many pioneer remedies for mushroom poisoning; none of them works. Seek immediate medical attention.

I once met a gang of tree planters who'd eaten the wrong

mushroom and tried to counteract the poison by drinking grain alcohol. It didn't work.

I had to leave when they started howling at the ravens.

That's why if you want to pick mushrooms, go for chanterelles. With their golden color, meaty caps, and fluted stems, chanterelles are easy to identify. They make the domestic store-bought mushroom taste like the cardboard box it came in.

Chanterelles can cost a dozen dollars a pound in the city. This may seem expensive for a common mushroom that grows almost anywhere there's second-growth timber. Not if you factor in the price of fuel to trash your rig stump jumping in the mushroom woods in the first place. Multiply that with the legal cost of picking the wrong mushrooms in the wrong place without a permit, times the medical expense of getting your stomach pumped from eating the wrong mushroom, and the price of chanterelles seems reasonable.

Picking chanterelles can be one of the best ways to get out and enjoy the fall woods. It's like the biggest Easter egg hunt in the world. It is an uncanny coincidence that picking chanterelles is like picking blackberries. Many of the best patches are on top of hornet or yellow jacket nests. You were warned.

Picking chanterelles has become very competitive now that people are doing it for money. Once you've found your secret mushroom patch, chances are it won't be a secret for long.

Cut the chanterelles with a knife. Carry them in a basket or bucket so that they won't get squished, no matter how long it takes to get back to the road.

Mushroom picking is one of the very best ways to get lost. It's easy to get turned around, walking through the woods with your eyes on the ground, scurrying from one mushroom patch to the other in the failing autumn light. That's when I always seemed to find the best mushroom patch. But often when lost in the mushroom woods at night, I've paused to reflect: chanterelles are worth whatever they cost.

Misery of Migration

We've all heard of the epic flights of migrating waterfowl flying from the Arctic Circle to the tropics and back without fail every year. It is a wonder of nature to observe the great flights of geese, ducks, and cranes arranged in precise V's, flying blade-straight and steel-true to a location somewhere else.

Then there are the other birds—the throwbacks that couldn't keep up with the rest of the flock. These were the ones I seemed to attract to the mountain pond. It was the misery of migration.

Those birds were late, lonely, and looking for a meal. I tried to help these lost souls continue on their journey with corn and leftover junk food. It seemed to have the opposite effect. Some of these migrating birds became so well adjusted to their new surroundings they wouldn't leave.

I worried about enabling the birds or endangering their health by subjecting them to the rank leftovers of a human diet. Then I would see some feathered friend pecking at a soggy hotcake on a frozen dawn and know I'd done the right thing.

Like the mourning dove that flew in that November morning. The poor thing should have been in Mexico enjoying a tropical vacation by now. Instead, it was lost in a frozen swamp in the wilderness with a flock of the worst sort of birds, the Canada jays.

A.K.A. the camp robber or whiskey jack, the Canada jay is a voracious pest that becomes more obnoxious the longer you feed them.

It was sad to see the slim, elegant mourning dove adopted into a flock of morbidly obese camp robbers and sinking to their level. Normally, feeding the birds through a hard winter would be considered an act of kindness to our feathered friends, unless the birds are Canada Jays.

Camp robbers are scavengers who can fly off with about half their own weight in pancakes and stash them in the trees for later. Their beaks are as sharp as a dagger. Watching them tear into a frozen carcass is a chilling experience if you consider these cheery little birds would probably just as soon peck away at your carcass if you lay still in the snow long enough.

Feeding a pack of camp robbers is like having a flock of hyperactive mini-vultures constantly circling your house, demanding more. It's a cycle of abuse. Fill your birdfeeder with a quality feed and you'll attract desirable species. Use your birdfeeder as a garbage disposal and you deserve anything that flies in.

The only thing worse than feeding the camp robbers are the blue jays they hang out with. Also known as the stellar jay to those who care, the blue jay has a call that sounds like a dying animal in pain, except if they were dying, they would eventually be quiet. Inevitably, the noise of the feeding jays will attract the ravens. The appearance of ravens at your birdfeeder could be a sign of a more serious problem. It's like having buzzards roost on your house. If you have ravens at your birdfeeder, maybe you should consider some spring cleaning or going to the dump a little more often.

Ravens are a highly intelligent life form with the ability to lift the lid off a garbage can. The ravens have a language all their own. After years of study, I was able to translate much of it. The ravens are making fun of us.

While many of the birds seemed unwilling to migrate any further, I couldn't see how a lot of them made it this far on their epic journey.

Grebes, for example. Grebes are a primitive form of diving bird.

Their legs are short and set too far back on the body. Their wings and tail are almost too small for flying. A grebe has to taxi a long way, kicking their ridiculous lobed toes to get airborne. Once aloft, the grebe flies as if it's looking for a place to crash.

This is liable to happen since grebes have been known to mistake wet pavement for water. Landing on pavement can be a rough break for a grebe since they need water to take off.

When alarmed, grebes swim in circles making little whistling sounds. This makes for an amusing display, but it's not migration. It's easy to look down your nose at the poor grebe, but if species went extinct just for being dumb, I think there are a lot of us that would be in trouble.

Just because a bird can fly doesn't mean its going anywhere. The sandhill crane is a majestic bird about the size of a great blue heron, famed for the length of its migration. The sandhill cranes' migration would not be such a long journey if they didn't waste so much time soaring around in circles while making a ridiculous call that sounds like a goose gargling beer.

This circling draws more cranes to the flock until it decides to fly a few more miles and start circling all over again. Then the white-fronted or specklebellied geese follow the sandhill cranes.

The geese spent the summer nesting in the muskeg, eating bugs, herbs, berries, and grasses. They molted and grew a whole new set of flight feathers. When the first storms of autumn hit the nesting grounds, the myriad species tested their wings and headed on down the Pacific Flyway. It's like a bird superhighway from the Arctic Ocean down the west coast of North America.

The journey starts easily enough. The choice is clear. To the north lies the vast expanse of ocean leading to the North Pole. To the south, the land stretches to the horizon. Rivers run through it. The geese ascend the rivers and cross the divide. They fly down other rivers on the other side, into the drainage of the Yukon.

Crossing the Yukon, the birds work their way up the tributaries into the heights of the coast range.

Beyond these mountains, there is the open expanse of the Pacific Ocean. From here south, the migration must be easy to navigate. By keeping the land to their port (left), and the ocean starboard (right), the way south is obvious. Flying between thirty-five and forty miles an hour, the geese can travel hundreds of miles a day even without a tail wind.

It's not until the birds reach the northern entrance to the Strait of Juan de Fuca that the real navigation problems start.

Flying south from Vancouver Island, the birds are surrounded by water on three sides. Crossing the strait, the prevailing westerly winds push the birds east along a narrow, inhospitable bench of flatland between the mountains and the sea.

There is very little along the shore of the Strait of Juan de Fuca that resembles a friendly patch of muskeg to land in. They have just flown thousands of miles with nothing to eat but a scrap of seaweed. Going further south would mean a turbulent climb of an eight thousand-foot hump of inedible rock formed by the Olympic Mountains. That prospect seemed to be enough to send the geese flying back north again. Their calls echoed through the hills. I used to love the calls of the geese at night. These poor birds were hungry, tired, and lost.

One morning the specklebellies spotted a meadow and a pond with my great blue heron standing on the edge of it. The geese dropped through a hole in the clouds and landed on the pond. Then waddled up through the pasture and began feeding.

I walked out to get a look at the specklebellies. Old Bill was standing there, not spooked, so the geese acted like they hadn't seen a human being before to be afraid of one. It would have been no problem to get a goose dinner, except of course Old Bill would never have spoken to me again.

The old market hunter recommends you shoot the leader of a flock. Geese mate for life, so the rest of them will circle back to see what's wrong. It's a dirty trick to get a chunk of meat that's tougher than your grandma's army boot, but it's better than no meat at all. After while I was able to get close enough to see what the geese were feeding upon so eagerly. Elk pellets.

All thoughts of a goose dinner faded.

One morning, there was a very unusual goose on the pond. I called him Bob. He was a little subspecies of Canada goose about the size of a mallard with a dark coloration—that made him a dusky cackler.

These are so rare they are not legal to hunt. Bob must have sensed this. He liked people, but then he'd probably never seen one before.

Bob liked to go for walks, or sit and talk and look at the sky. I spent a lot of time doing the same thing, so we got along pretty well. Bob was such a skinny little thing, I started to worry about his diet. All he ate was grass and bugs that were almost too small to see. I thought he should try to bulk up if he was going to have a chance of flying south over the mountains.

I tried feeding Bob corn and junk food out of the bird feeder but he wouldn't have any of it. Canada geese really are smart birds. I considered loading him into a pet carrier to drive him south, but that would have been a vacation. That's not a migration either.

One night as the moon rose over the misty swamp, a flock of geese was passing by. Something told me the little goose would join them. In the morning, Bob was gone. I wished him Godspeed.

The Winter Wren

One day in November at noon
The wren had me into her room
For vapors and cider and something to eat
She on her perch and I on my seat.

These winter woods are lonely
I've often heard it said
That everything that lived here
Has flown away or dead.

But far beneath the eternal din
Of wind and sleet and hail
The winter wren has settled in
To tell her cheery tale.

"I follow a faint trail
From dawn until the light should fail
Till darkness draws the final veil
To end this winter evening's tale
I am small but I am old
I've grown accustomed to the cold
The wind that reaps the tallest tree
Cannot harm the likes of me
Though devils stalk these woods by night
I've a song at morning's light."

Crows and Owls

It was daylight in the swamp after a dark and stormy night. I thought the wind would blow the roof off the shack, but it didn't. You wonder how anything could live through a night like that in the woods, with the wind howling and the trees blowing over, but they do.

The crows are the first things to wake up. A lot of people don't like crows, but I do. The crows spend their winter days raiding the valley, being a nuisance to nearly every living thing.

As dusk descends, the crows think it wise to hide for the night somewhere far away from where they spent the day. Small groups of crows begin flying to the foothills to roost. These flocks gather until they look like a giant black amoeba in the sky. The roosting flock can be miles long. One night I counted over a thousand crows in one flight, and I missed a lot of birds.

That many crows make a lot of noise. The leaders fly in erratic patterns until they select a roost. Once the leaders start circling, the rest of the crows gather into a black tornado that melts into the timber. Then the crows are silent.

Inevitably, stragglers come cawing from over the horizon. How these latecomers keep track of the flock is anyone's guess. The roosting crows are silent and invisible, but the late crows fly straight to the roost with telepathic accuracy.

It is an eerie feeling to be in the woods where the crows are sleeping. The roosting area can cover several acres. The crows are tucked so tightly in the branches, they are almost impossible to see. They don't fly away or even move when you walk beneath them in the twilight. This is odd because crows are normally afraid of people. When night comes on, there's something in the woods far more terrifying to the crow than a human being—the great horned owl.

Crows spend their lives making other animals miserable. Cats, hawks, and people are all fair game, but the crow's favorite fun is to gang up on an owl.

The owls hunt at night and roost during the day, so it's fun to watch the crows work out on a roosting owl. Twilight puts the shoe on the other foot. When night comes, the crows sleep and the owl comes out to hunt them.

The great horned owl is a fearsome predator. Standing almost two feet tall, with a three-foot wingspan, it can take off and fly away with a full-grown rabbit like it was nothing. I know that now.

I remember seeing the owl in the middle of the road one night, standing on a big rabbit. The owl was looking at me with those big eyes like "you'd better find another road." I don't know why I thought I could catch the owl in my coat. I wanted to turn it loose in the house to hunt mice.

I noticed the owl's talons sunk into the rabbit, his beak the size of a pickaxe. The big saucer-shaped eyes stared right at me. Suddenly, grabbing the owl for a pet was not such a good idea. I was relieved when it lifted off and flew away with the rabbit.

On a good night, the owls start calling about the time the crows go to bed. The little screech owl sounds like a drunken teakettle. The boreal owl has a call like someone pounding a steel wedge. When the great horned owl hoots, all the other owls go quiet. Nothing answers a great horned owl but another great horned owl. Once you get the stereo owls tuned up, they sound like foghorns in love. The crows huddled on their branches. There was terror in the night. I shut the door and lit a lamp.

Winter

That winter was a hard one
Long nights of ice and wind
Short days of indecision
The storm was moving in.

It blew down from the mountain
And beat upon the door
For days I gave up counting
Till I could bear no more.

In that hour before the dawn
The earth was frozen and forlorn
The Star of Morning brightly shone
Upon eternal hope reborn.

Cougars

I didn't mean to teach the ducks how to ski. Even with the best of intentions things can happen that we later feel responsible for. There's no going back. That winter was a hard one. The pond was frozen and covered with snow. The creek that ran into the pond ran off a little waterfall that kept an area about the size of a wading pool from freezing over.

It grew colder. Every evening, thousands of mallards flew up the river into the mountains. They were looking for gravel and drinking water to digest their evening meal.

I dumped a sack of corn on top of a snow bank about ten feet above the pond and stood back. It only took a day or so for the birds to find it. Hundreds of ducks came circling in through the blizzards to have a feed at the pond.

The ducks liked to land in the water and then waddle up the hill to the corn. Of course, the ducks were wet when they came out of the pond. They dripped water on the way up the hill. Soon the trail to the corn was icy and slick.

A big hen mallard launched herself at the top of the slide and skied down to the pond for a perfect two-point landing. Soon there was another and another and then a line of ducks doing the same thing, skiing to the bottom of the hill and then marching back up with a little wing assist to do it again.

It was fun watching the ducks ski. I thought about timing their downhill runs and maybe putting in a slalom course, when I realized it was the cabin fever talking.

Then there arose a commotion. All of the ducks except one flew off with a roar of wings and tumultuous quacking. The remaining duck was pinned under the grip of a bald eagle. I thought if anyone deserved a duck dinner, it was me: I bought the corn.

By the time I put on my snow boots, the eagle and the duck were gone. I packed some more corn out to the pond. That's when I noticed something added to my tracks in the snow from that morning—large, fresh cougar prints following mine. I suddenly felt a long way from home.

I dumped the corn at the top of the ski run. There was a lot of blood and feathers from the unfortunate duck, but more ducks were already circling back for a feed or a ski run or both. I dumped the corn and retreated inside to the stove.

Many people have lived their entire lives in the woods without seeing a cougar. They are shy and elusive animals. Cougar sightings are often so brief the only thing you remember is a furry streak with a big tail.

Every once in a while, I'd hear a growl or a scream in the night and figured "Kitty" had just ended another deer's garden-raiding career.

Right before the big snow, Kitty killed a deer at the edge of the yard. That was another mess I didn't want to have to deal with. I went to town. When I returned home, the deer was half-eaten. The next morning, there was nothing left of the deer but some green stuff and a pile of hair. I never caught a glimpse of the cat.

The next morning the ducks piled into the pond by the hundreds. There was a waiting line at the ski run.

I had better things to do than watch the ducks ski. It was snowing again and colder than a witch's collection agency. I was busy keeping the stove going. Then all the ducks took off from the pond. Something had frightened them.

I bundled up and walked outside. Something had gotten into my boat. It was like a hurricane had struck.

My boat always had the smell of success with the aroma of fish, fish eggs, and shrimp. From the tracks, I guessed Kitty must have gotten hungry. Somehow, she got into the boat and tangled up in some fishing line. I blamed myself. It looked like I needed a new landing net. That was a bad kitty. Cougar tracks led off through the snow. They were going my way, so I followed them down a trail through the woods to get my mail. It had stopped snowing. There was no fresh snow in the cougar tracks. I thought I must have been getting closer to Kitty when she ducked down into a brushy canyon. I got the mail and headed back up the trail. Again, there were cougar tracks on top of mine. Kitty was following me everywhere. It was a feeling like I was never really alone.

I called to the cat several times, but there was no response. I walked home with an eye on my trail.

Back at the pond, the ski run was deserted. Tracks in the snow told the story: a cougar had crept within forty feet of the ski run, made a couple of tremendous leaps, and caught a drake mallard in the air.

I thought it must have been another cougar eating the ducks, since Kitty was busy stalking me at the time.

There were more feathers and blood being covered with snow. The weather got colder until the creek and the remaining open water in the pond froze. The corn was covered overnight with two feet of fresh powder. The ducks quit coming around.

Bucky the Elk

It's a sad day when you read about the death of a friend in the newspaper. He had been involved in a hunting incident. The subsequent operation was successful, but he was not expected to live. Those of us who knew him were not surprised by the tragedy. His life was like a train wreck a long time coming.

Born on the remote headwaters of the Dungeness River, Bucky the Elk began life as an average calf with his then-single mom in the vicinity of Avalanche Canyon. Bucky was far from average. He was born inside Olympic National Park, which made him a United Nations World Heritage Biosphere Reserve elk.

Bucky had a promising career ahead of him as a government elk being studied by a team of government biologists. By the time he'd reached adolescence, it was clear that a National Park just wasn't big going to be big enough for Bucky.

One hard winter, he migrated down from the mountains with the rest of the herd. There below, on the shore of the Strait of Juan de Fuca, lay the Sequim Prairie.

Sequim was a S'Klallam Indian word for quiet waters. Once upon a time, the Sequim Prairie had been a 1,500-acre savannah grassland. It was always good hunting country. In 1977, the Manis Mastodon site was discovered near the Sequim Prairie. Archaeologists uncovered a broken spear point at the site that was stuck in a mastodon rib bone about fourteen thousand years ago. This is the oldest documented human activity in the Pacific Northwest.

The mastodon were furry prehistoric elephants that might have stood ten feet tall at the shoulder. The males had curved tusks that could be fifteen feet long. The Manis mastodon was killed in a pond at the end of the last Ice Age. The landscape was different then. The climate was warmer and drier. There were grasslands with willows and cattails near water. The forests had yet to sprout from the recently glaciated landscape. The people hunted mastodons, mammoth, bison, and caribou until the extinction of these Pleistocene Megafauna about ten thousand years ago.

At about six thousand years ago, the coniferous forests began to appear. The Native Americans maintained prairie grasslands throughout the West by burning them every three to five years. The fires kept the forests from taking over. Regular burning killed plant diseases, pests, and bugs, and kept the dried brush from accumulating and making the fires so hot they might kill the plants.

It has been estimated that more than eighty different plant species were gathered for roots, berries, tubers, and bulbs that were used as food, tools, medicine, charms, and cosmetics.

Camass bulbs may have been the most important source of carbohydrate staple. It was second only to dried salmon as a trade commodity. The camass (pronounced like campus, without the p) is a small member of the lily family with a blue hyacinth-shaped flower and a bulb about the size of garlic. Camass plots were owned, maintained, and passed down through generations of families. The bulbs were gathered by digging with sharpened sticks in early summer after the blue blossoms had died. The camass gardens were cleared of weeds and rocks. The sod was lifted out in small sections so that the largest camass bulbs could be removed. For storage, the bulbs were steamed in communal stone or earth ovens and then pressed into loaves. Lewis and Clark referred to these loaves as a type of bread. The Corps of Discovery tried eating camass when they had exhausted their food supply. The expedition was nearly stopped by an overpowering side effect of this new diet—debilitating flatulence, "which filled us so full of wind we were scarcely able to breathe."

In May of 1792, Captain George Vancouver sailed his ship, *Discovery*, into the Strait of Juan de Fuca. The captain was so impressed with the beauty of the area, with its lawns and cleared areas, he named it Dungeness after his home in England.

In 1861, James Swan described vast numbers of deer and droves of elk on the Sequim Prairie. Swan advised anyone hunting in Sequim that meat should be packed off the prairie by dark or it would be eaten by wolves before morning.

The Sequim elk were market hunted for sale just across the Strait of Juan de Fuca in Victoria where the Hudson Bay Company turned the elk into pemmican, a staple mixture of dried, pounded meat and dried fruit bound with fat that fed the fur trade.

The coming of the timber industry increased the demand for elk meat. Even if you didn't care for elk, it was a nice change from the usual logging camp fare of beans and sowbelly.

By the 1880s, the elk herds were driven off the Sequim Prairie. Lieutenant Joseph P. O'Neil's 1885 expedition into the high eastern Olympics reported large herds of tame elk that had yet to be hunted. By 1900, these same elk were almost eradicated for their meat and ivory teeth, which made dandy watch fobs. Elk hunting season was closed in 1905. The wolves and the bears were bounty hunted. Varmint hunting became a popular career for all the out-of-work market hunters.

In 1909, President Teddy Roosevelt preserved the central portion of the Olympic Mountains as an Elk National Monument. This later became what is now Olympic National Park. With no predators or hunting seasons, the Olympic elk reached the capacity of their range. Elk hunting season was reopened.

The surviving Sequim elk retreated up the Dungeness and Greywolf rivers to the sanctuary of the thick brush in the deep canyons.

Meanwhile, the Sequim Prairie was being settled. In 1851, the first Europeans appeared on the beach at Dungeness. The Homestead Laws allowed pioneers to settle unclaimed lands. The Native

American's camass gardens and prairies were seen as unclaimed land. Their crops were weeds and brush to the homesteaders.

In 1853, John W. Donnell was the first settler on the Sequim Prairie. Water was scarce. He found a species of prickly pear cactus growing. He raised grain and turned the hogs loose to plow up the camass. In the 1880s, a plague of grasshoppers ate everything down to the fence rails.

With the miracle of the first irrigation ditch in 1896, the Sequim Prairie blossomed into a dairy farming community, leaching manure into the Dungeness River while pumping fish onto the fields for fertilizer.

By 1996, the farmers were being removed by a new breed of settler, the retirees. They flocked to the rain shadow of the Olympics and filled in the farmland with housing developments. It was like my good old uncle Joe used to say, "One acre of farmland paved over is a tragedy, a thousand acres is a statistic."

Sequim became an Indian word for traffic jam. The people of Sequim liked to drive around with little dogs on their laps, causing the rest of us to ask, "Please, let the dog drive."

The economy boomed. Sequim became a worker's paradise of tract homes, trailer parks, and box stores so thick they blocked my view of Wal-Mart.

Roads, subdivisions, and office complexes were named after the elk and other wild creatures that could no longer survive in Sequim.

At the time, you could hardly think of a more hostile environment for an elk herd except for one thing—elk hunting was again outlawed. This was a lucky break for the elk. By the 1990s, the Dungeness elk herd had been reduced to about twenty head. How the elk learned of their new legal status one day and moved into the town the next was a mystery to some.

Elk hunters have long held that the more intelligent elk are able to read the hunting regulations. Reading may have been one of Bucky's proudest accomplishments, we'll never know. He took that secret to the grave.

Once the elk moved to town it didn't matter how they got there. There were no cougars or poachers in Sequim, just a few yapping dogs and shrieking gardeners. Retired people love to garden. Bucky loved to eat. His antlers grew and grew to outlandish proportions on a secret diet of lavender. Some said he spent entirely too much time growing and polishing his antlers, but none of that mattered to Bucky. He was pursuing his dream of becoming an elk model. During his career, he posed for photographers and modeled for the bull elk sculptures at the entrances to Sequim.

Friends who knew Bucky said he was a leader who devoted his life to helping others and breaking down barriers. It's not that Bucky couldn't jump a fence. That was not his style. He simply put his head down and helped the entire herd right through the fence. Bucky was known to wear a strand of barbed wire in his antlers just for show. It was a fashion statement other elk copied.

Bucky also enjoyed pruning rose bushes, fruit trees, and ornamental shrubs in neighborhood gardens all over Sequim. He never charged a dime for his services.

Bucky had his critics. Some said his antlers went to his head. In the celebrity world of model elk, size does matter. In no time, Bucky was making the scene with a large, exclusively female entourage that kept growing with the size of his antlers.

The sudden celebrity status put Bucky in the spotlight. Unfortunately, the spotlight had some crosshairs in it. Bucky had to worry about stalkers.

The Sequim elk had become a problem. By the dawn of the twenty-first century, the elk and human populations had undergone an explosion in growth that threatened water quality, traffic safety, and the future of sustainable agriculture in Sequim.

An elk-removal solution was suggested. I proposed an alternative, based upon sound scientific principles, to measure the impact of each species on the environment.

It was said that the elk affected water quality. If you ever watched a herd of elk stand in the middle of the Dungeness River, you'd know that. It's disgusting, but nothing compared to the failed human septic tanks that have fouled the Dungeness River and the bay it runs into. That was one for the elk.

There is no question the elk were a danger to traffic safety. When the elk herd crossed the highway, wrecks occurred caused by people pulling over to watch. That could be dangerous, but when was the last time an elk drank a six-pack of beer and passed you on a blind corner? That's two for the elk.

The elk were accused of threatening sustainable agriculture. I remember when the elk herd walked through my garden. Talk about instant mashed potatoes! Then the elk went away. I could plant again.

Once the humans move into your garden, they'll compact the soil with heavy machinery and cover it with gravel, pavement, or buildings so that it will never grow food again. That's three-nothing elk.

Suggested possible solutions to the elk-human conflict included birth control, fencing, and relocation.

While many methods of birth control have been available for years, the human population continues to explode.

Building a fence sounded like a good idea, but when we tried to build a fence on our southern boarder with Mexico, we needed illegal aliens to do it.

Relocation of the elk was attempted with disturbing results. The elk were shot with dart guns out of a helicopter, loaded onto trucks, and paroled to other unsuspecting communities. A wild elk is a dangerous animal. A wild elk on drugs is even more dangerous. The relocated Sequim elk taught the rest of the elk bad habits, like pruning roses and fixing fences.

My alternative proposed the relocation of the Sequim humans. Many of these humans were already on drugs. They could have been lured onto a bus with more drugs. Then whisked away to the evil cities across the water and released into a crowd, say after a baseball game or a rock concert where they could blend with the locals.

Instead of implementing these modest proposals, elk hunting was proposed to limit the population of the elk herd. Hunting the Sequim elk was some of the toughest hunting there was. The elk were accustomed to living in housing developments full of people who were liable to shoot back.

I proposed the reintroduction of the Olympic timber wolf to

control the elk population. The howling of the wolf is a true symbol of the wilderness. I could think of no better way to restore nature's balance than to return the wolf to the Sequim Prairie.

Of course no one suggested that people be forcibly removed from their homes for wolf habitat. It was naturally assumed that once homeowners found themselves surrounded by packs of hungry wolves, they would become willing sellers.

The Olympic timber wolf was known to attack people. In June of 1916, Forest Ranger Chris Morganroth was treed by a pair of wolves near the Lillian River. After the experience, he said of the wolves, The "revolver has the same value in the Olympics as on the Texas border."

With the restoration of the Olympic timber wolf, there would only remain one endangered species missing from the environmental mosaic that was the Sequim Prairie: the bull trout.

The Sequim Dungeness Valley is not a valley. It is a delta of alluvial deposits that eroded from the Olympic Mountains eons before there were any loggers to blame. With each flood, the Dungeness becomes a river of stone. During high water, you can hear the boulders pounding in the river as they spill out of the mountains and settle into the slower current, piling the sediments higher.

Once the sediments reached a certain height, the river has roamed from one channel to another across the delta since the last Ice Age. Since the river was contained within dikes, the bull trout has not been free to roam.

With the removal of the dikes and a corresponding release of the sediment load, the Dungeness River would be free to reclaim its former delta, which includes the city of Sequim and its surroundings. It might be a real improvement for Sequim if a river ran through it.

The unobstructed Dungeness River channel would have reclaimed valuable bull trout habitat. That, along with a program of wolf reintroduction and regular burning of the Sequim Prairie would have restored the elk herds and the fragile ecosystem that drew visitors to Sequim in the first place.

Unfortunately, instead of demonstrating a basic sense of

responsible, environmental stewardship, the government reopened the Sequim elk-hunting season.

On that fateful opening day, Bucky stopped his morning antler polishing and stepped out to pose once more for his picture as the official Sequim Mascot. He was gunned down instead.

Those of us who knew Bucky were deeply saddened at the news of his untimely passing.

With Bucky gone, Sequim wasn't the same. There was too much asphalt. There was no room for wild life. Bucky the elk had to go and so did I.